You Say I'm a Bitch Like It's a BAD Thing

You Say I'm a Bitch Like It's a BAD Thing

TEN SPEED PRESS
Berkeley | Toronto

Ed Polish * Darren Wotz

Ten Speed Press
Box 7123
Berkeley, California 94707
www.tenspeed.com

Distributed in Australia by Simon and Schuster Australia, in Canada by Ten Speed Press Canada, in New Zealand by Southern Publishers Group, in South Africa by Real Books, and in the United Kingdom and Europe by Airlift Book Company.

Cover design by Betsy Stromberg
Text design by Betsy Stromberg and Ed Polish

Library of Congress Cataloging-in-Publication Data

Polish, Ed.
    You say I'm a bitch like it's a bad thing / Ed Polish, Darren Wotz.
      p. cm.
      ISBN-10: 1-58008-637-3
      ISBN-13: 978-1-58008-637-0
      1. Advertising. 2. Humor in advertising.
3. Women in advertising. I. Wotz, Darren. II. Title.

HF5801.P55 2004
659.1'02'07--dc22

                        2004051695

Printed in China
First printing, 2004

9 10 11 12 13 – 09 08 07 06

Thanks to Victoria McOmie, Jack and Bess Polish, Julie Bennett, Ben Truwe, Ray Guadagnino, Jeff Errick, and the gang at Ephemera, Inc.

Check out Ephemera, Inc. at
www.ephemera-inc.com

Explain to Me Again Why I Need a Man

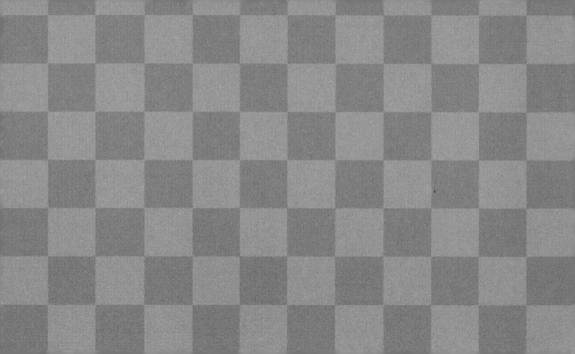

I understand the concept of COOKING & CLEANING, just not as it applies to me.

DRINK COFFEE

Do Stupid Things Faster
with More Energy!

YOU GO
GIRL

...AND TAKE
THOSE
TACKY SHOES
WITH YOU

You Mean
Shopping
for More
Useless Crap
Isn't the
Meaning of Life?

Mommy,
when I grow up
I want to be
a total bitch
just like you.

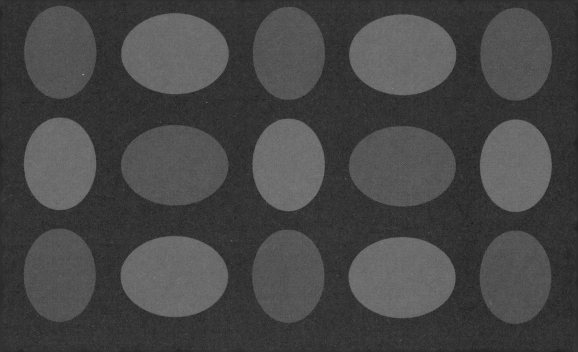

Men Are Like Coffee

The Best Ones Are Rich, Warm, and Can Keep You Up All Night Long

OPPOSITES ATTRACT

and then they drive each other insane

I Had Sex With My Husband & All I Got Was This Lousy Kid

AMAZINGLY ENOUGH,

I DON'T GIVE A SHIT.

Don't
Assume
I'm Not Into
Cheap,
Meaningless
Sex

THE FIRST
40 YEARS OF
PARENTHOOD
ARE ALWAYS
THE HARDEST

BEHIND EVERY GREAT WOMAN

Is A Man Checking Out Her Ass

Queen of
Fucking
Everything

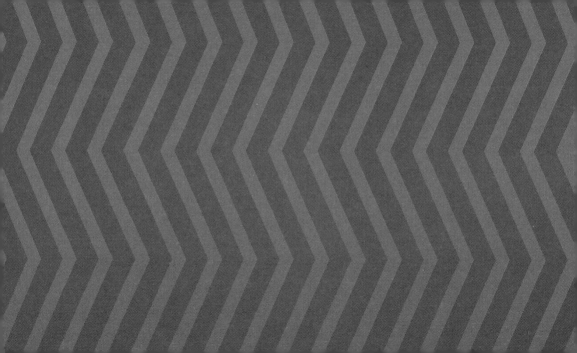

COFFEE
ISN'T
HELPING.
GET THE
JUMPER
CABLES.

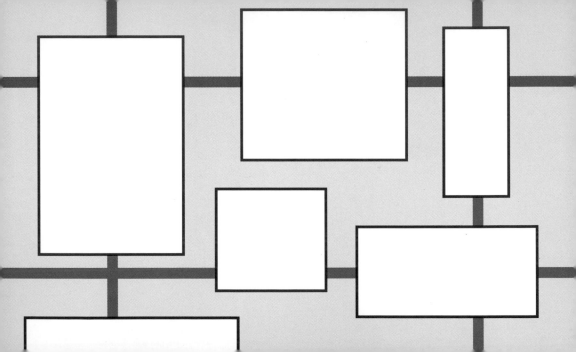

BEING
UNSTABLE
& BITCHY
IS ALL
PART OF MY
MYSTIQUE

**Admitting You're
An Asshole Is
The First Step**

"STRESSED"
is
"DESSERTS"
spelled
backward

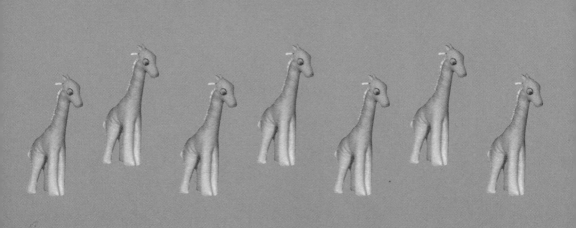

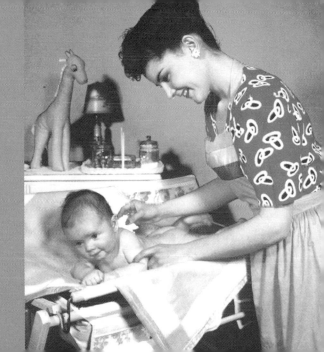

BE NICE TO YOUR KIDS—

They'll Choose Your Nursing Home

I never met a man I couldn't blame.

I only fake it so he'll buy me stuff.

I WANT IT ALL...

AND I WANT IT SMOTHERED IN WHIPPED CREAM AND CHOCOLATE

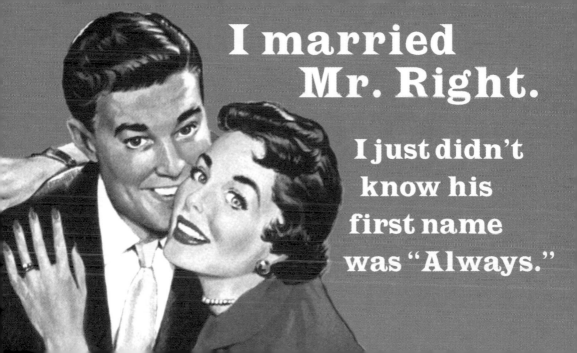

Easy there,
Mr. Testosterone—
You can
be replaced
by a zucchini.

Can't...
think....
Blood...
rushing...
to...penis.

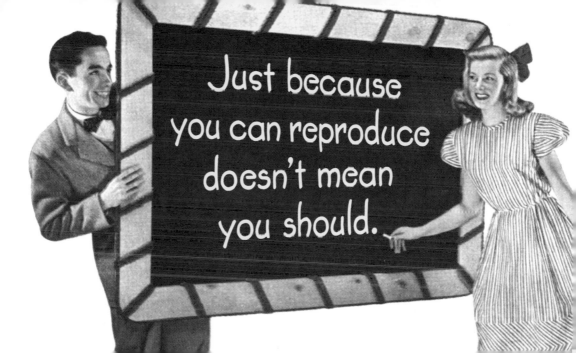

I Don't Cook, Clean, or Put Icky Things Near My Mouth.

MAKE YOURSELF AT HOME!

CLEAN MY KITCHEN

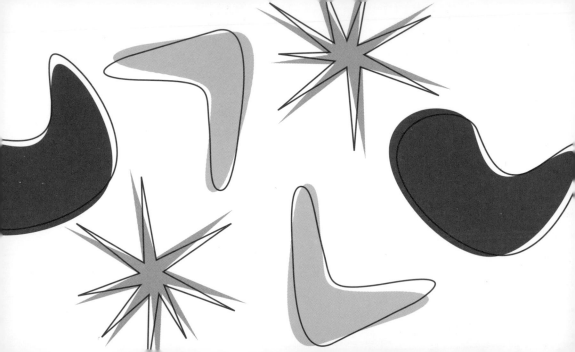

CHILDREN ARE A BLESSING

You never know when you'll need blood or a spare kidney.

Babe

In

Total

Control of

Herself

HOW COME ALL THE COOL GIRLS ARE LESBIANS?

Ask Me About A Fabulous Career In Bitching

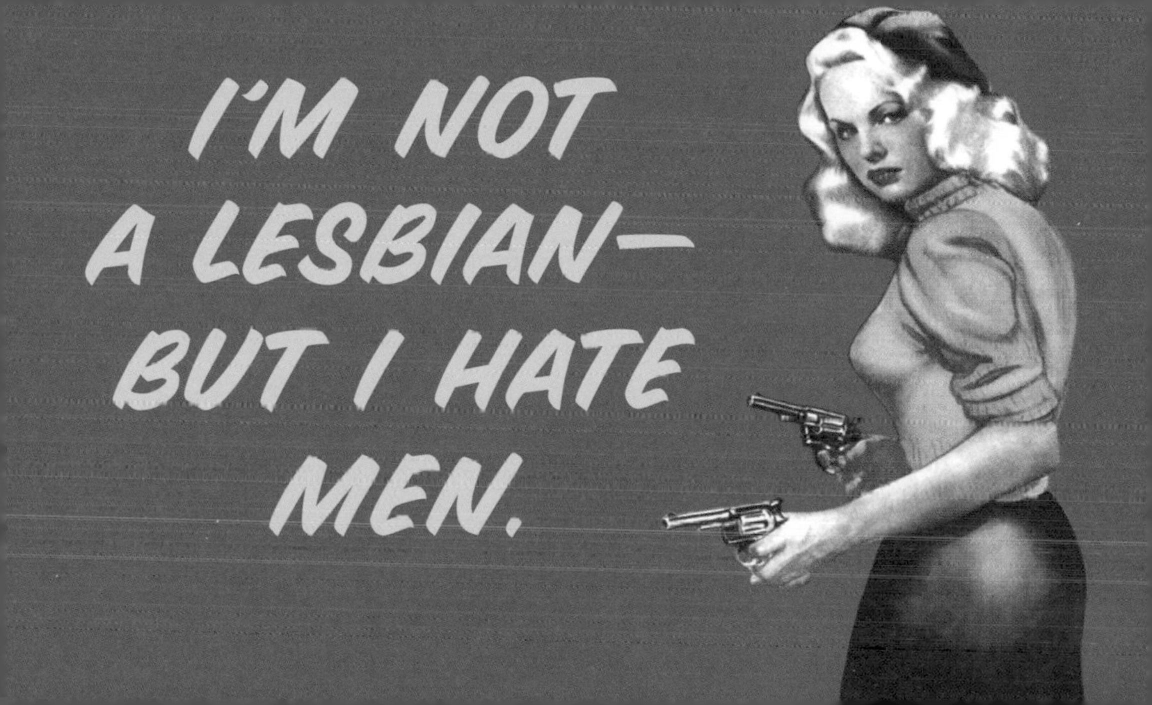
I'M NOT
A LESBIAN—
BUT I HATE
MEN.

I HAVEN'T HAD MY COFFEE YET

DON'T MAKE ME KILL YOU

So Much To Do
So Few People
To Do It For Me

I gave up
jogging because
my thighs kept
rubbing together
and setting my
pantyhose
on fire.

I'm Having My Period and Can Therefore Legally Kill You

MEN ARE LIKE
FLOOR TILES...
If You Lay Them Right
The First Time You Can
Walk All Over Them
For Years!

I used
to care
but now
I take
a pill
for
that.

IT'S BEEN LOVELY BUT I HAVE TO SCREAM NOW

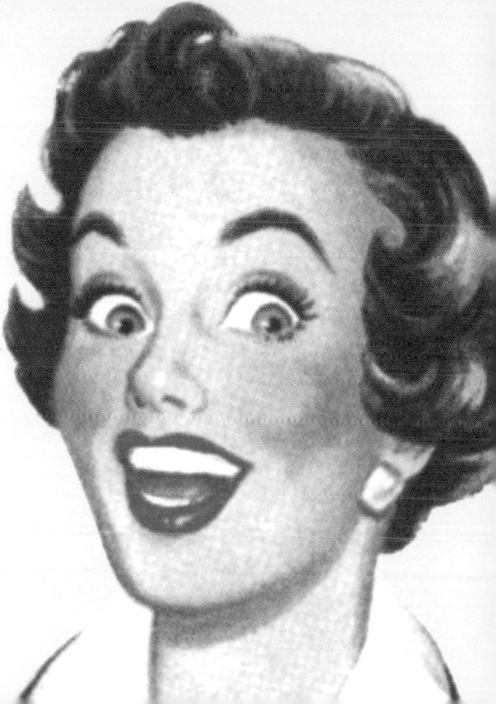

ABOUT THE AUTHORS

ED POLISH is the owner of Ephemera, Inc., a novelty company specializing in buttons, refrigerator magnets, and other products. Ed never apologizes for his art and he does his own nude scenes. He lives in Ashland, Oregon, with his wife, Victoria.

DARREN WOTZ does his best to appear productive to the untrained eye. Sarcasm is just one of the services he offers. He lives in Berkeley, California, and New York City.